W9-BJS-678

Nature's Children

BOAS

John Woodward

GROLIER

FACTS IN BRIEF

Classification of Boas

Class: *Reptilia* (reptiles)
Order: *Squamata* (lizards and snakes)
Family: *Boidae* (boas and pythons)
Subfamily: *Boinae* (boas); *Erycinae* (sand boas)
Genus: Eight genera in *Boinae* and three in *Erycinae*.
Species: 23 to 25 species in *Boinae* and 12 in *Erycinae*.

World distribution.   Mainly Central America and South America. Also United States, Africa, southern Asia, and New Guinea.

Habitat.   Mainly damp forests, rivers, lakes, and swamps. Also warm deserts and oceanic islands.

Distinctive physical characteristics.   Big and bulky snake. Most have eyes with vertical-slit pupils. Small "spurs" at base of tail.

Habits.   Some live in forest trees. Others hunt on the ground or in water. Desert boas burrow underground by day.

Diet.   Usually hunt live animals. Prey varies from mice and lizards to deer and alligators. Tree-climbing boas often catch birds.

© 2004 The Brown Reference Group plc
Printed and bound in U.S.A.
Edited by John Farndon and Angela Koo

Published by:

**An imprint of Scholastic
Library Publishing
Old Sherman Turnpike, Danbury,
Connecticut 06816**

Library of Congress Cataloging-in-Publication Data

Woodward, John, 1954–
  Boas / John Woodward.
    p. cm. — (Nature's children)
  Includes index.
  Summary: Describes the physical characteristics, habits, and natural environment of various species of boa constrictors.
  ISBN 0–7172–5957–9 (set)   ISBN 0–7172–5959–5
   1. Boa (Genus)—Juvenile literature. [1. Boa constrictor. 2. Snakes.] I. Title. II. Series.

QL666.O63W66 2004
597.96'.7—dc21
                                        2003049164

Contents

Some people think all snakes are venomous (poisonous). But many snakes have no venom, including the boas. The boas are a fascinating group of snakes. The smallest are barely 20 inches (50 centimeters) long. The biggest are the largest snakes in the world, more than 30 feet (9 meters) long.

Boas don't kill with venom. They kill their prey by squeezing the breath out of them. Boas wrap themselves around their victims—then squeeze until they suffocate their prey. This technique is called constriction. One of the most common kinds of boa is called the boa constrictor. Nearly all boas kill by constriction, not just boa constrictors.

Some boas live on the ground or in the water, while others climb trees. Many are vividly colored and patterned. But they are all expert hunters, and many have senses that help them pinpoint their prey.

Boas like this Colombian rainbow boa are very strong, with great muscular coils.

What Is a Boa?

There are at least 35 different species of boa. The boas are very like another group of snakes called the pythons. Pythons and boas belong to the same scientific family, called the Boidae, which sounds like "boy-day."

Like boas, pythons are powerful snakes that kill their victims by squeezing. Both groups of snakes include some real giants. But most pythons live in Asia and Africa and lay eggs. Most boas, on the other hand, live in the Americas and give birth to live young.

Like all snakes, boas have very long, thin bodies. But most boas are much thicker and more muscular than other snakes. The exceptions are tree boas, which are quite slim. Boas have broad, flat heads, too. Unlike many other snakes, they have a definite neck.

This African rock python is one of the boas' cousins from Africa. Like boas, it kills by constriction.

Where Do Boas Live?

Most boas live in the hot, steamy rain forests of Central and South America. The heat suits them, and there is plenty for them to eat. Many boas live and hunt on the forest floor. Many boas are also good swimmers, and some live all the time in the water of rivers, lakes, or swamps. Others live up in the trees, where they ambush birds and other tree-living animals.

A handful of boa species (types) live in forests outside the Americas. Three live in the forests of New Guinea and nearby islands. Three more live on the island of Madagascar, off southern Africa.

Some boas don't live in forests at all, but in dry places where there is plenty of sand. There are sand boas like this in the dry regions of Africa and Central Asia. They burrow into the sand by day and come out to hunt at night.

North America also has two kinds of boa of its very own: the rosy boa in the southwestern deserts and the rubber boa in the cool conifer forests of the American west and northwest.

Opposite page:
If you want to meet a boa, go to a tropical swamp. There you may well see one slithering in and out of the water, waiting to catch prey.

Little and Large

Many boas are quite small. The rosy boa of Mexico and the deserts of the southwestern United States grows to about 40 inches (100 centimeters) at most. The sand boas of Africa and Asia are no bigger. The Pacific ground boa of New Guinea is even smaller. This ground boa has a fat, heavy body, but grows barely 18 inches (50 centimeters) long.

Yet some boas are simply gigantic. Boa constrictors can grow to 13 feet (4 meters), and maybe longer. Even that is small compared to the colossal green anaconda. Green anacondas live near the steamy rivers of the Amazon Basin in South America. Most are well over 16 feet (5 meters) long. Some grow up to 30 feet (9 meters) and weigh as much as three football players—more than 550 pounds (250 kilograms). They are quite simply the heaviest snakes in the world. And only reticulated pythons are anything like as long.

Not all boas are big. This East African sand boa is barely 1 yard (1 meter) long.

Scaly Skin

Boas are reptiles, and like all reptiles, they have dry, scaly skin. The scales are not separate plates, like those of many fish. They are simply hard studs that are part of the skin. Sometimes, they overlap like tiles on a roof. The boa's scales act like a flexible armor. They also help keep the snake from drying out. That is important for the sand boas that live in very dry places.

As a boa slides over the ground or through trees, its scaly skin gets worn and damaged. So, like all snakes, the boa regularly sheds the outside layer of its skin. That reveals a new one that has grown underneath. The old skin is rolled off the snake's body in one piece, like a sheet of wrinkled plastic. Even the skin covering its eyes comes off. The boa emerges looking brighter and more colorful. People used to think that old snakes actually became younger when they shed their skins!

Opposite page:
A boa's body is covered in scales that overlap like the tiles on a roof. These scales belong to a green tree boa.

Inside a Boa

A boa's body is supported by a long backbone made of hundreds of small bones called vertebrae. The backbone is strong but very flexible, like a bike chain. All the joints are controlled by powerful muscles, so the boa can wriggle around or hold itself in a rigid coil around its prey. Rib bones attached to the backbone protect the boa's heart, lungs, liver, and other internal organs. They are all elongated to fit inside its long, slender body. Most snakes save space by having only one working lung, but a boa has two.

The really strange thing about a boa is the pair of small spurs near the back of its body. The distant ancestors of all snakes were lizards with four legs. Over millions of years these animals lost their legs and evolved (developed) into snakes. The boa's spurs are all that is left of its ancestors' back legs.

*The tiny claw shape in the middle of this picture is
a boa's spur—the last trace of its ancestor's legs.*

Cold-blooded?

Animals have to be warm to work properly. If they are too cold, their muscles seize up, and they cannot digest their food. Animals such as birds, cats, and people make sure this never happens by having central heating systems. So they are "warm-blooded" even in winter. But like all reptiles, including other snakes, lizards, and turtles, boas have no central heating. They are naturally "cold-blooded." That means they rely entirely on the heat of the sun to keep them warm.

That may sound like a bad arrangement, but in the tropics—where most boas live—it is no problem at all. The tropical climate is so warm that boas are more likely to get too hot. And they do not waste energy running central heating systems. So they need far less food than warm-blooded animals of the same size.

Boas like this emerald tree boa can sleep a lot because they don't waste energy finding food just to keep warm.

Sun and Shade

Opposite page: *Like other boas, boa constrictors bask in the sun to warm up if they're cold, or if they need extra energy for hunting.*

To stay fit, an animal must not only stay warm, but it must also stay at just the right temperature. Warm-blooded mammals and birds have natural "thermostats" that keep their temperatures tightly controlled. A thermostat controls the heat that a central heating system produces.

Boas can put up with a much wider variation in temperature than people can. But even they need to get it roughly right. Although they have no thermostat, they manage this by basking in the sun if they're cold or slipping into the shade or cool water if they overheat. In cooler parts of the world they have to bask in the morning to warm up. But in the tropics the sun can be too hot, so many tropical boas are active at night and hide by day. In deserts with hot days and cold nights sand boas emerge to hunt at twilight, when the temperature is just right.

Gliding and Looping

It's hard to imagine getting around without legs, but a boa manages so well that legs would probably just get in the way! When a boa is not in a hurry, it can inch its way along using the big scales on its belly. It moves each scale forward, hitches it over a rough bit of ground, and pulls it back. That pulls the snake forward. While some scales are moving back, others are moving forward, so the boa glides along like a slug. Giant boas like the anaconda use this method nearly all the time.

A smaller boa can move faster by pushing against plants and stones with loops of its body, rather like a swimming eel. Many boas can also swim just like eels. This method works up in the trees, too. Tree boas also get around by gripping branches with their tails and stretching forward in an extending zigzag.

Opposite page:
Tree boas move through the treetops like other boas swim through water. A tree boa simply grips a branch with its tail and zigzags to the next branch.

Ears and Eyes

Opposite page:
To avoid being dazzled during the day, a boa's eyes narrow to slits like the eyes of a cat.

Like all snakes, boas are deaf. Or rather, they have no true ears. Yet they have their own very sensitive equipment for listening to vibrations. These listening devices are connected to the boa's lower jawbone. A boa often lies with its jaw against the ground or a branch. That way it can probably "hear" things like the thud of footsteps some way away—giving it plenty of time to slip into hiding.

A boa's eyes work better than its ears, but a boa cannot see much detail and rarely notices things that do not move. Yet the eyes of a night-hunting boa can open up very wide at night. That lets in a lot of light so the boa can see quite well in the dark. During the day the eyes narrow to slits like the eyes of a cat. The boa probably uses its eyes when attacking prey, but relies on other, more acute senses to find prey in the first place.

A boa finds its prey by tasting the air with its forked tongue for lingering traces of the prey's scent.

Tasting the Air

Boas find their prey with their acute senses of taste and smell. Indeed, a boa lives in a world of smells and tastes. A large section of its brain is devoted just to detecting and identifying them. The boa's brain is linked by nerves to a pair of nostrils and to a cavity in the top of the snake's mouth called the Jacobson's organ. This organ is sensitive to all kinds of chemicals, which the boa gathers using its forked tongue.

As it glides along, a boa constantly flicks its tongue in and out through a notch in its upper lip. The tongue picks up tiny particles of scent floating in the air. When the boa pulls its tongue in again, it curls the forked tip up into the Jacobson's organ. Sensors in the Jacobson's organ pick up the scent particles from the tongue. The information travels up the nerves to the boa's brain, which then identifies the scent. Following chemical signals like these, the boa can track its victims wherever they go.

Seeing the Heat

Opposite page:
Boas can find their victims even in complete darkness. They detect their victim's body heat with the pits along their bottom lip.

All snakes can hunt their prey by taste and scent. But many night-hunting boas have a remarkable extra sense. With that sense they can locate warm animals in complete darkness, using heat detectors in pits on their lips. The heat sense is shared by only a few other types of snakes, including pythons and rattlesnakes.

The heat detectors work much like the "snooperscopes" used by police helicopters to follow criminals in the dark. The pits pick up invisible infrared (heat) rays from warm objects, including warm-blooded animals like mice, squirrels, and birds. To a boa a mouse seems to glow in the dark as if lit up from inside. So once the boa has tracked its victim by scent, the boa has no trouble "seeing" where its prey is and launching an attack.

Boas lie so still they're hard to notice. This frog may be unaware it could soon become a boa's dinner.

What Do Boas Eat?

Like all snakes, boas eat only meat, which they usually find by hunting. Small boas often prey on lizards and frogs, but larger boas prefer furry, warm-blooded mammals, such as mice and rats. The bigger the snake, the bigger the animals it can eat. The giant anaconda has been known to eat small pigs, small deer, and even alligators!

Night-hunting boas with heat sensors always target warm-blooded mammals and birds because their warm glow makes them easy to detect. An Amazon tree boa can see the glow of a roosting bird in pitch darkness and snatch it from its perch with deadly accuracy. Other boas, like the rainbow boa, often eat bats, creeping into caves to seize them while they sleep.

Ambush!

Opposite page: *Emerald tree boas ambush their prey in the branches— then slowly tighten their coils around the unlucky animal.*

Boas sometimes go on the prowl in search of prey, but mostly they sit and wait for their victims to come to them. They can afford to wait a long time because they don't need to eat very often. Cold-blooded animals don't use up their energy keeping warm; so if they stay still, they can survive on very little food. Some big snakes like the boa constrictor can go for months without eating at all.

Many boas specialize in ambush tactics. The emerald tree boa drapes itself over a branch up in a rain-forest tree, taking a tight grip with its muscular tail. If an animal or bird comes within range, the boa can spring forward, snatch its victim, and kill it—without moving from its favorite perch.

Tight Squeeze

A boa always catches its prey with its teeth. The snake may not be venomous, but its teeth are long and sharp. The teeth of bird-killing tree boas are particularly long so they can pierce the thick feathers of their prey. The teeth also curve backward like hooks. So when a boa gets its teeth into its unfortunate victim, it has absolutely no chance of escape, no matter how much it struggles.

Once it has a grip with its teeth, a boa may just swallow its prey alive. But usually it kills the animal by constriction. The boa quickly throws a few coils of its body around its prey's body, then tightens the coils like a noose.

Every time its victim breathes out, the snake tightens its grip a little more, so the trapped animal cannot breathe in again. Before long the snake's victim goes limp and dies. It is not crushed to death, but slowly suffocated.

Outsized Mouthful

Boas swallow their victims whole. That may not seem surprising until you remember that most of their victims are much bigger than the boa's head. Imagine trying to swallow a whole pumpkin, and you have some idea what it's like for a snake!

A boa can manage this feat because its jawbones are only loosely attached to its skull and to each other. That allows the snake to stretch its mouth around its victim like elastic. The boa grips its monster mouthful with the hooked teeth on one side of its lower jaw, maybe the left side. Then it moves the jawbone on the right side forward. It gets another grip, unhooks the left side, and moves that forward again. So, bit by bit, the boa drags its mouth over its meal. Eventually, it squeezes the whole lot down its throat. It always swallows its prey headfirst so it slips down more easily.

Anacondas are so strong even a caiman—a cousin of the alligator—can fall victim to the snake's mighty coils.

The Mighty Anaconda

The biggest boa by far is the green anaconda, which lives in the swamps and rivers of tropical South America. It is a good swimmer and can stay underwater for up to 10 minutes at a time. It often lies beneath the water's surface waiting for prey in places where other animals come to drink, then grabs them and pulls them under to drown. If they struggle, the anaconda loops its huge body around them and suffocates them. An anaconda can kill wild pigs and deer like this. Anacondas have probably killed a few people this way, too.

The anaconda usually hunts by night and spends the day lying in the shallows or draped over the branches of a waterside tree. It can climb well and uses trees as safe refuges from other hunters—although it takes a fearsome killer to make a meal of an anaconda.

Confusing Colors

Opposite page: *Forest boas are masters of disguise. The patterns on their skin can make them very hard to spot among the trees.*

Really big boas like the anaconda and boa constrictor don't have many enemies apart from human hunters. But the smaller ones are sometimes eaten by crocodiles and alligators, big monitor lizards, and even other snakes. They are also attacked by eagles like the Guianan crested eagle. To protect themselves, boas are camouflaged with colors that make them hard to see. That also hides them from their victims, making it easier for them to spring an ambush.

Some boas are the same color as their surroundings. Up in the forest trees the green skin of the emerald tree boa makes perfect camouflage. Others, like the boa constrictor, have confusing patterns that disguise their shape. A few, like the dazzling rainbow boa, glitter with rainbow colors as they move—but no one knows how that helps them survive.

Although bright red, this Amazon tree boa's color matches the bromeliad (a tropical plant) it is on.

Attracting a Mate

Boas normally live alone, but each year—or for big boas maybe once every two years—they get the urge to mate and have young. Just after shedding her skin, a female boa gives off an attractive odor called a pheromone. Any males in the neighborhood soon pick it up, follow the scent trail, and track her down.

Sometimes two males find the female at the same time, and there may be trouble. But eventually the weaker male backs down, and the stronger one has the female to himself.

Sliding alongside her, the male presses his body close to hers with his head resting on her neck. Then he uses his spurs to tickle her back and encourage her to mate. They intertwine their tails, and the male passes his sperm into her. Then they separate and slip away. The two may never meet again. The sperm carries the male's sex cells. When it meets the female's eggs—her sex cells—it fertilizes them. The two are now ready to develop into baby snakes.

Baby Boas

Female boas give birth to live young. That is uncommon among snakes. Pythons, for example, lay eggs. Big boas like the anaconda can have more than 50 babies at a time, but most have fewer than this. They try to have their young at a time of year when there is plenty of food for them to eat, such as in the tropical rainy season. But if the weather is cold, the babies take longer to grow inside their mother, so they are born late. A boa constrictor can be pregnant for five to eight months depending on her body temperature.

Baby boas are like tiny versions of their parents. A newborn anaconda is only about 2 feet (60 centimeters) long, while its mother is typically more than 16 feet (5 meters) long. Yet the baby boa can look after itself almost right away and is soon off hunting entirely alone for small animals.

Most snakes hatch from eggs. Baby boa constrictors are born live and can soon fend for themselves.

Growing Up

Young boas leave their mother soon after they are born and live alone. Their mother doesn't teach them where to find prey or how to kill it. They just know from the first. And if they are not very good at it at first, they quickly get much better with practice.

At first, young boas eat only small animals. Young anacondas eat frogs and fish, and young tree boas eat insects and lizards. The more the boas eat, the quicker they grow. By about two years old young boas may be big enough to have babies of their own.

The real problem for young boas is not eating but being eaten. A small snake makes a tasty mouthful for a big animal—especially since a boa cannot defend itself with a venomous bite like other small snakes. That may be why young emerald tree boas are not green but reddish brown. They are harmless, but look just like deadly poisonous tree vipers, so other hunters leave them well alone.

Opposite page: *Young and old emerald tree boas hanging from a branch. Emerald tree boas are bright green when fully grown. But when they are young, they are reddish brown. That way the young look like deadly tree vipers, so other animals don't attack them.*

45

Boas and People

Many people keep boas as pets. The boa constrictor, emerald tree boa, rainbow boa, and rosy boa are particularly popular. Only those who really know what they are doing should ever take on a boa as a pet. But boas can do well if they are looked after properly and may even breed. Most of the boas sold in pet stores are bred like this, rather than being caught in the wild. Rare species like the Madagascan Dumeril's boa are also being bred in captivity. That may help them survive if their natural homes are destroyed.

Sadly, many boas are also killed every year for their beautiful skins. The main victims are the green anaconda, yellow anaconda, and boa constrictor. All these snakes are big enough for people to make bags and boots from their skins. So many of the snakes are shot that few get the chance to grow really big. The giant boas once described by early travelers now seem to be very rare indeed.

Words to Know

Basking Lying in the sun to warm up. Snakes do this a lot because their bodies do not work properly if they are cold.

Camouflage Colors and patterns that make something difficult to see by blending into the background.

Cold-blooded Describes a type of animal that relies on the temperature of its surroundings to keep it warm.

Constriction Killing an animal by squeezing it so hard that it cannot breathe.

Rib A curved bone that encloses and protects vital internal organs like the heart and lungs.

Sperm The male cells that fuse with female eggs to enable them to develop into baby animals.

Spurs The small claws near the tail of a boa or a python.

Thermostat A device that keeps something at a constant temperature.

Venom Poison injected by an animal to kill or paralyze another.

Vertebrae The bones that link together in a chain to form an animal's backbone or spine.

Warm-blooded An animal that can keep its body at the right temperature however hot or cold its surroundings is warm-blooded. Only mammals and birds are truly warm-blooded.

INDEX

Cover Photo: Nigel Dennis / NHPA
Photo Credits: Daryl Balfour / NHPA, page 4; Fritz Polking / Still Pictures, pages 7, 29;
Nigel Dennis / NHPA, pages 8, 16&17, 30; Winfried Wisniewski / Corbis, page 10; Michel
Gunter / Still Pictures, page 13; M. &. C. Dennis-Huot / Still Pictures, pages 18, 25, 42; Tom
Brakefield / Corbis, page 21; Dr Eckhart Pott / NHPA, page 22; Steve Robinson / NHPA, page
26; Gerard Lacz / NHPA, page 33; Peter Pickford / NHPA, page 34; Klein/Hubert / Still
Pictures, page 37; Anthony Bannister / NHPA, page 38; Robert Henno / Still Pictures, page
41; Albert & Jacqueline Visage / Still Pictures, page 45.